Midjourney AI: Enhancing Art, Not Replacing Artists

Written By Cloud Knight

Aka

Vincent Vento

All Rights Reserved

Chapter 1

In recent months, the world of art has seen a significant shift with the rise of "Midjourney AI", an artificial intelligence tool that creates art based on prompts. This tool has caused a stir in the art world, with many people concerned that AI will eventually replace traditional artists and their jobs. However, despite these concerns, the popularity of Midjourney AI continues to grow as more and more people embrace this new technology.

Midjourney AI uses advanced algorithms and machine learning to generate unique pieces of art based on a user's input. From paintings and drawings to sculptures and installations, Midjourney AI is capable of creating a wide variety of art forms. The tool has quickly gained a following among artists and non-artists alike, who are fascinated by its ability to produce original works of art in just a matter of minutes.

At first glance, it may seem like Midjourney AI is on its way to taking over the art world. However, as we will see in this book, the rise of this tool is not so simple. Midjourney AI may be changing the way art is created and distributed, but it is not necessarily replacing traditional artists or their jobs. In fact, as we will explore in the following chapters, Midjourney AI has the potential to enhance the art world and inspire artists in new and exciting ways.

Chapter 2

The topic of artificial art and its place in the world of traditional art has been a contentious issue for many years. On one hand, there are those who believe that AI-generated art represents a new frontier in creative expression and has the potential to push the boundaries of what is possible in the art world. On the other hand, there are those who argue that AI-generated art lacks the soul and emotion that makes traditional art so special, and that it threatens the livelihoods of traditional artists.

One of the biggest concerns about AI-generated art is that it may eventually replace human artists and take away their jobs. As technology continues to advance, it's not hard to imagine a future where machines can create high-quality works of art with ease, leaving human artists struggling to compete. This fear is compounded by the fact that AI-generated art is often faster, cheaper, and more efficient than traditional art, making it a more attractive option for many people.

Despite these concerns, it is important to understand that AI-generated art is still in its infancy and has a long way to go before it can truly replace human artists. While AI-generated art may be able to imitate certain styles and techniques, it is still not capable of truly understanding the nuances and complexities of human emotion. This lack of emotional depth is what sets human art apart and makes it so valuable.

It is also worth considering that AI-generated art has its own unique strengths and weaknesses. While it may not have the emotional depth of traditional art, it can offer a fresh perspective and new avenues of creative expression. For example, AI-generated art can be used to explore new forms and styles that are not possible with traditional art techniques. This can be especially useful for artists who are looking to push the boundaries of their own work and experiment with new approaches.

In addition to its potential as a tool for artists, AI-generated art also has the potential to democratize the art world. By making art accessible to a wider audience, AI-generated art has the potential to bring people together and inspire new forms of creative expression. This could be especially important for people who are not trained artists but still have a passion for art and creativity.

Of course, there are also those who argue that AI-generated art has no place in the world of traditional art. They argue that art should be created by humans, with all of their flaws, emotions, and imperfections, and that machines cannot replicate this human touch. While this is a valid perspective, it is important to remember that AI-generated art is still in its early stages and has a lot of room to grow and evolve. As technology continues to advance, it is possible that AI-generated art will eventually develop its own unique qualities and become something truly special.

In conclusion, the topic of AI-generated art is a complex and controversial one, with valid arguments on both sides. While it may seem like AI-generated art is a threat to traditional artists, it is important to remember that it also has the potential to enhance and inspire the art world in new and exciting ways. As AI-generated art continues to evolve, it will be interesting to see how it will impact the world of traditional art and what role it will play in shaping the future of the art world.

Chapter 3

One of the biggest concerns about the rise of AI-generated art is the fear that it will lead to job loss for traditional artists. With machines capable of creating high-quality works of art in a matter of minutes, many artists are worried that their skills and talents will become irrelevant in a world dominated by technology. This fear is not unfounded, as many industries have already been impacted by automation and artificial intelligence.

However, it is important to understand that AI-generated art is not yet advanced enough to completely replace human artists. While AI may be able to imitate certain styles and techniques, it is still not capable of truly understanding the complexities and nuances of human emotion. This lack of emotional depth is what sets human art apart and makes it so valuable.

In addition, there are many aspects of the art world that machines simply cannot replicate. For example, human artists bring their own experiences, perspectives, and emotions to their work, which is something that AI-generated art cannot do. This is what gives traditional art its unique qualities and makes it so special.

While there is certainly a risk of job loss for traditional artists, it is not yet clear how significant this impact will be. There is still a lot of room for growth and development in the world of AI-generated art, and it is possible that new opportunities will arise as technology continues to advance. For example, as AI-generated art becomes more prevalent, there may be a growing demand for human artists to help refine and perfect these machine-generated works.

It is also worth considering that the rise of AI-generated art may not necessarily lead to job loss for traditional artists, but rather to a shift in the types of jobs available in the art world. For example, as AI-generated art becomes more prevalent, there may be a growing demand for artists to help refine and perfect these machine-generated works. Additionally, there may be a growing need for artists to help educate the public about AI-generated art and its place in the world of traditional art.

Another factor to consider is the impact that AI-generated art may have on the art market. As more people embrace this new technology, the value of traditional art may change, which could have a significant impact on the livelihoods of traditional artists. While this is a valid concern, it is important to remember that the value of art is subjective and that there will always be a market for human-created art, regardless of the rise of AI-generated art.

In conclusion, while the rise of AI-generated art may lead to job loss for traditional artists, it is not yet clear how significant this impact will be. It is important to understand that AI-generated art is still in its early stages and has a lot of room to grow and evolve. As technology continues to advance, there may be new opportunities for traditional artists to remain relevant and valuable in the art world. It is also important to remember that there will always be a market for human-created art, regardless of the rise of AI-generated art.

Chapter 4

One of the main reasons why traditional art will always be valued over AI-generated art is because of the power of human creativity. Human artists bring their own experiences, perspectives, and emotions to their work, which is what makes each piece of art unique and special. This emotional depth and personal connection are something that AI-generated art cannot replicate, no matter how advanced it becomes.

Creativity is not something that can be programmed or taught, it is an innate human quality that sets us apart from machines. Human artists can express their thoughts, feelings, and ideas in ways that are complex, nuanced, and emotional. This is what gives traditional art its immense value and beauty.

Art has the power to move us, inspire us, and connect us in ways that technology cannot. It could evoke powerful emotions, communicate important messages, and leave a lasting impact on those who experience it. This is something that AI-generated art will never be able to achieve.

Additionally, human artists can use their creativity to push boundaries, explore new ideas, and experiment with new techniques. They are not limited by the algorithms and data sets that govern AI-generated art but are free to create in any way they see fit. This freedom of expression is what makes traditional art so dynamic and exciting.

While AI-generated art may be impressive, it will never have the same emotional impact as traditional art created by a human artist. This is because AI-generated art is created based on data sets and algorithms, rather than personal experiences and emotions. It may be able to imitate certain styles and techniques, but it will never be able to truly understand the complexities and nuances of human emotion.

In conclusion, the power of human creativity is what sets traditional art apart from AI-generated art. Human artists can express their thoughts, feelings, and ideas in complex and emotional ways that machines simply cannot replicate. This emotional depth and personal connection are what gives traditional art its immense value and beauty, and will ensure that it remains relevant and valuable in the world of art.

Chapter 5

Another reason why traditional art will always be valued over AI-generated art is because of the beauty of imperfection. Human artists are not perfect, and their work reflects this. Each piece of traditional art is unique and special, not only because of the creativity and emotion that goes into it, but also because of the imperfections that make it one-of-a-kind.

Imperfections give traditional art its character, depth, and authenticity. It makes it real, human, and relatable. AI-generated art, on the other hand, is perfect in a way that can be perceived as cold, sterile, and artificial. Its perfection is a result of algorithms and data sets, rather than the creativity and emotion of the artist.

The beauty of imperfection can also be seen in the creative process of traditional art. Human artists often embrace the unknown, embrace their mistakes, and use them to create something new and unique. This is what makes traditional art so dynamic, unpredictable, and exciting.

Moreover, the beauty of imperfection also adds a layer of emotional depth to traditional art. Imperfections can evoke powerful emotions, communicate important messages, and leave a lasting impact on those who experience it. They are a reminder that we are all human, and that life is not always perfect. This emotional depth and connection are something that AI-generated art will never be able to achieve.

In conclusion, the beauty of imperfection is one of the key reasons why traditional art will always be valued over AI-generated art. Imperfections give traditional art its character, depth, and authenticity, and make it real, human, and relatable. AI-generated art may be perfect in its own way, but it will never have the same emotional impact as traditional art, which is the result of the creativity, emotion, and imperfections of the human artist.

Chapter 6

One of the most important reasons why traditional art will always be valued over AI-generated art is because of the emotional connection that it creates between the artist and the audience. Human artists can use their own emotions, experiences, and perspectives to create art that speaks to the human condition in ways that AI-generated art simply cannot.

Art has the power to move us, inspire us, and connect us in ways that technology cannot. It could evoke powerful emotions, communicate important messages, and leave a lasting impact on those who experience it. This emotional depth is what gives traditional art its immense value and beauty.

Art can bring people together and create a sense of community and belonging. It allows us to share experiences, perspectives, and emotions, and helps us to understand and connect with each other in ways that are both profound and meaningful. This emotional connection is something that AI-generated art will never be able to achieve.

Moreover, the emotional connection that traditional art creates between the artist and the audience is also an important factor in the creative process. Human artists often draw on their own experiences and emotions to create their work, which is what makes each piece of art unique and special. This emotional depth and personal connection are what sets traditional art apart from AI-generated art.

In conclusion, the emotional connection between the artist and the audience is one of the most important reasons why traditional art will always be valued over AI-generated art. Human artists are able to use their own emotions, experiences, and perspectives to create art that speaks to the human condition in ways that technology cannot replicate. This emotional depth and personal connection are what gives traditional art its immense value and beauty, and will ensure that it remains relevant and valuable in the world of art.

Chapter 7

As AI continues to evolve, it is becoming increasingly clear that there is a role for collaboration between artists and AI. Rather than seeing AI-generated art as a threat to traditional art, many artists are beginning to view AI as a tool that can help them to push the boundaries of their art and create new and exciting works.

One way that artists can collaborate with AI is by using AI tools, like Midjourney AI, to generate basic compositions, which they can then build upon using their own creativity and skills. This can help artists to explore new ideas and perspectives and can inspire them to take their art in new directions.

Another way that artists can collaborate with AI is by using AI algorithms to generate new art styles and techniques. By working with AI, artists can explore new ways of creating art, and can find new and innovative ways of expressing their creativity.

Collaboration between artists and AI also has the potential to bring new audiences to the world of art. AI-generated art can attract new and younger audiences who might not have been interested in traditional art and can introduce them to the beauty and creativity of the art world.

Moreover, collaboration between artists and AI can also help to break down the barriers between the art world and the technology world. By working together, artists and AI can create new and exciting forms of art that merge the best of both worlds.

In conclusion, as AI continues to evolve, it is becoming increasingly clear that there is a role for collaboration between artists and AI. Rather than seeing AI-generated art as a threat to traditional art, many artists are beginning to view AI as a tool that can help them to push the boundaries of their art and create new and exciting works. By collaborating with AI, artists can explore new ideas, perspectives, and art styles, and can attract new and younger audiences to the world of art.

Chapter 8

Despite the differences between traditional art and AI-generated art, it is important to acknowledge that AI can also be a source of creative inspiration for human artists. AI tools, like Midjourney AI, can help artists generate new ideas and perspectives, and can provide a new way of looking at the world.

Artists can use AI-generated art as a starting point, and then build upon it, adding their own creativity and emotions to create something truly unique. AI-generated art can serve as a source of inspiration, a new way of seeing the world, and a means of pushing the boundaries of traditional art.

For example, an artist might use Midjourney AI to generate a basic composition, and then use their own skills and creativity to build upon it, adding their own style, color choices, and emotional depth. In this way, AI can be a tool that helps artists to explore new ideas, perspectives, and styles, and can help them to take their art in new and exciting directions.

Moreover, AI-generated art can also serve as a way of pushing the boundaries of traditional art. It can inspire artists to think outside the box, challenge themselves, and experiment with new techniques and styles. By exploring the possibilities of AI-generated art, artists can grow and evolve as artists, and can find new ways of expressing themselves and their creativity.

In conclusion, while there will always be a distinction between traditional art and AI-generated art, it is important to acknowledge that AI can also be a source of creative inspiration for human artists. AI tools like Midjourney AI can help artists generate new ideas and perspectives, and can serve as a means of pushing the boundaries of traditional art. By using AI as a tool for creative inspiration, artists can continue to grow and evolve as artists, and can find new ways of expressing themselves and their creativity.

Chapter 9

As AI-generated art continues to gain popularity and prominence, the question of how to prepare future artists for this new reality is becoming increasingly important. Art education will play a crucial role in shaping the future of the art world, and in helping artists to navigate the changing landscape of art and technology.

One of the key changes that is likely to take place in art education is a greater focus on technology and AI. In the future, it will be important for artists to have a basic understanding of AI, and to be able to use AI tools, like Midjourney AI, as part of their creative process. Art schools will need to adapt and update their curriculums to include courses on AI, machine learning, and other related subjects.

Another change that is likely to take place in art education is a greater focus on collaboration between artists and AI. Art schools will need to teach students how to work with AI, how to use AI tools, and how to incorporate AI into their art. They will also need to encourage students to explore the possibilities of AI-generated art, and to find new and innovative ways of using AI in their work.

Additionally, art education will also need to focus on the human elements of art, such as creativity, emotion, and connection. As AI-generated art continues to evolve, it is important that artists can create works that are not just technically impressive, but also emotionally engaging and meaningful. Art schools will need to help students develop their emotional intelligence, creativity, and intuition, and to help them understand the importance of connecting with their audience.

Finally, art education will also need to focus on the ethical implications of AI-generated art. As AI-generated art becomes more prevalent, it is important that artists can understand the ethical and moral issues that arise, and to make informed decisions about how they use AI in their work. Art schools will need to incorporate discussions of ethics into their curriculums, and to help students understand the impact that AI-generated art can have on the world.

In conclusion, the future of art education will be shaped by the changing landscape of art and technology. Art schools will need to adapt and update their curriculums to include courses on AI, machine learning, and other related subjects. They will also need to encourage students to explore the possibilities of AI-generated art, and to find new and innovative ways of using AI in their work. Additionally, art education will also need to focus on the human elements of art, such as creativity, emotion, and connection, and on the ethical implications of AI-generated art. By preparing future artists for the challenges and opportunities of the AI age, art education will play a crucial role in shaping the future of the art world.

Chapter 10

As AI-generated art becomes more prevalent, it is also starting to have a significant impact on the art market. This new form of art is challenging the traditional way of buying and selling art, and it is causing many people to question the value of AI-generated art.

One of the biggest challenges that AI-generated art is facing in the art market is the issue of authenticity. Unlike traditional art, which is created by a human artist, AI-generated art is created by a machine. This raises questions about the value and authenticity of AI-generated art, and it makes it difficult for buyers to know what they are buying.

Another challenge that AI-generated art is facing in the art market is the issue of scarcity. Traditional art is unique and one-of-a-kind, but AI-generated art can be created in unlimited quantities. This makes it difficult for buyers to see the value in AI-generated art, as it is easily replicable and does not have the same level of scarcity as traditional art.

Despite these challenges, the art market is also starting to see some of the benefits of AI-generated art. One of the biggest benefits is the democratization of art. With AI-generated art, it is possible for anyone to create and sell art, regardless of their background or experience. This has the potential to level the playing field and to make the art market more inclusive.

Another benefit of AI-generated art is its accessibility. With AI-generated art, it is possible to create large quantities of art quickly and inexpensively. This makes art accessible to a wider range of people, and it has the potential to increase the size of the art market.

The art market is also starting to see some new and innovative business models emerge. One of these new business models is the use of AI-generated art as a form of investment. Some people are using AI-generated art to diversify their portfolios and to invest in a new and exciting asset class.

Despite the challenges and benefits of AI-generated art, the art market is still trying to figure out how to deal with this new form of art. As AI-generated art continues to evolve, it is likely that the art market will continue to change and adapt to this new reality.

In conclusion, AI-generated art is having a significant impact on the art market. The art market is facing many challenges, such as the issue of authenticity and scarcity, but it is also seeing many benefits, such as the democratization of art and the accessibility of art. As AI-generated art continues to evolve, it is likely that the art market will continue to change and adapt to this new reality.

Chapter 11

As AI-generated art becomes more prevalent, it is also starting to raise ethical questions. The use of AI to create art raises important questions about creativity, ownership, and the value of art. These ethical questions are complex, and they require us to consider a wide range of issues.

One of the main ethical questions that arise from AI-generated art is the issue of creativity. Is AI-generated art truly creative, or is it just an imitation of human creativity? Some people argue that AI-generated art is not truly creative because it is created by a machine and does not reflect the unique thoughts and experiences of a human artist.

Another ethical question that arises from AI-generated art is the issue of ownership. If a machine creates a piece of AI-generated art, who owns the rights to that art? Some people argue that the machine that created the art should own the rights to the art, while others argue that the person who programmed the machine should own the rights to the art.

The issue of value is another ethical question that arises from AI-generated art. If AI-generated art can be created in unlimited quantities, does it have the same value as traditional art? Some people argue that AI-generated art has a lower value because it is easily replicable, while others argue that AI-generated art has a higher value because it is created by a machine and is therefore unique.

In addition to these ethical questions, AI-generated art also raises important questions about the role of the artist in society. Some people argue that the use of AI to create art is taking away the jobs of traditional artists and that it is reducing the importance of artists in society. Others argue that the use of AI to create art is increasing the importance of artists, as it is challenging artists to find new and innovative ways to create art.

One of the biggest ethical challenges that AI-generated art is facing is the issue of bias. Some AI systems are programmed with biases that can result in the creation of biased AI-generated art. This raises important questions about the responsibility of the creators of AI systems to ensure that their systems are free of biases.

Another ethical challenge that AI-generated art is facing is the issue of accountability. If something goes wrong with an AI-generated art piece, who is responsible for the consequences? Some people argue that the creators of the AI systems are responsible for the consequences, while others argue that the users of the AI systems are responsible for the consequences.

In conclusion, the rise of AI-generated art is raising important ethical questions that require us to consider a wide range of issues. From questions about creativity and ownership, to questions about the value of art and the role of artists in society, the ethical questions that arise from AI-generated art are complex and they require us to think deeply about the future of art. As AI-generated art continues to evolve, it is important that we continue to consider the ethical implications of this new form of art.

Chapter 12

The rise of AI-generated art has brought the concept of originality to the forefront of artistic discourse. In the digital age, where information is easily accessible and software can generate endless variations of images, the idea of originality is becoming increasingly complex. The question of what constitutes original art is a contentious one, and the answer is not straightforward.

In the traditional sense, originality refers to the idea that an artwork is unique and created by the artist's own hand. This idea of originality has been a fundamental aspect of the art world for centuries. However, the rise of AI-generated art has challenged this concept of originality, as art can now be created by machines with little or no human intervention.

Some people argue that AI-generated art is not truly original because it is created by a machine and does not reflect the unique thoughts and experiences of a human artist. They argue that originality is an essential aspect of art, and that AI-generated art cannot be considered truly original because it is not created by a human.

On the other hand, some people argue that AI-generated art can be considered original because it is unique and cannot be replicated exactly by any other machine or human. They argue that originality is not just about the process of creation, but also about the outcome of that process. In this sense, AI-generated art can be considered original because it creates unique images that are not possible through any other means.]

The concept of originality is further complicated by the fact that AI-generated art can often be a collaborative effort between the machine and the human. For example, an artist may use an AI system to generate images that are then modified and refined by the artist. In this case, it can be argued that art is a combination of human and machine creativity and therefore original.

Another aspect of the debate surrounding the concept of originality in the digital age is the issue of copyright. If an AI system creates a piece of art, who owns the rights to that art? Some people argue that the machine that created the art should own the rights to the art, while others argue that the person who programmed the machine should own the rights to the art. This is a complex issue that is still being debated, and there is no clear answer yet.

In conclusion, the concept of originality in the digital age is a complex issue that is being debated by artists, art lovers, and legal experts alike. While some people argue that AI-generated art cannot be considered truly original because it is not created by a human, others argue that AI-generated art can be considered original because it creates unique images that are not possible through any other means. As AI-generated art continues to evolve, it is likely that the debate surrounding the concept of originality will continue, and it will be important for artists, art lovers, and legal experts to consider this issue and find a way to navigate the complexities of the digital age.

Chapter 13

In a world where AI-generated art is becoming increasingly prevalent, the value of the human touch in art is becoming more apparent. While AI systems can generate beautiful and intricate images, they lack the emotional and personal connection that is present in art created by human artists.

One of the key elements of human touch in art is the artist's individual experiences, thoughts, and emotions. An artist's work reflects their life, and the emotions and experiences that they have had. When someone looks at an artwork, they are not just seeing the image, but they are also seeing the artist's interpretation of the world.

In contrast, AI-generated art is created by algorithms and computer programs, and it does not have the same emotional connection that human-created art has. While AI-generated art can be beautiful and intricate, it lacks the personal touch that is present in human-created art.

Another aspect of the human touch in art is the artist's individual technique and style. Every artist has their own unique style, and the way they create their art is as unique as their fingerprints. This individual technique reflects the artist's personality and is what makes their work unique.

In contrast, AI-generated art is created by algorithms and computer programs, and while it can generate beautiful images, it lacks the personal touch that is present in human-created art. AI systems can generate endless variations of images, but they lack the individual style and technique that is present in human-created art.

The human touch in art is also important for the emotional connection that it creates between the artist and the audience. When an artist creates an artwork, they share a part of themselves with the world. The audience can feel this connection when they look at the artwork, and they can feel a sense of empathy with the artist.

In conclusion, the human touch in art is an important aspect of the art world, and it is something that AI-generated art cannot replicate. While AI systems can generate beautiful and intricate images, they lack the emotional and personal connection that is present in human-created art. The human touch in art is what makes art unique and special, and it is something that will always be valued in the art world.

Chapter 14

In a world where AI-generated art is becoming increasingly prevalent, the importance of the art-making process is becoming increasingly apparent. The process of creating art is just as important as the final product, and it is through this process that the artist can express their emotions, thoughts, and experiences.

One of the key elements of the art-making process is the time and effort that the artist puts into creating their work. When an artist creates an artwork, they are investing time and effort into the project, and this investment is reflected in the final product. The process of creating art is not just about creating a final product, but it is also about exploring and learning as the artist creates their work.

In contrast, AI-generated art is created by algorithms and computer programs, and the process of creating the artwork is not as important as the final product. AI systems can generate images quickly and efficiently, but they lack the time and effort that is put into creating human-created art.

Another aspect of the art-making process is the artist's individual technique and style. When an artist creates an artwork, they use their unique technique and style to create their work. This individual technique reflects the artist's personality, and it is what makes their work unique.

In contrast, AI-generated art is created by algorithms and computer programs, and while it can generate beautiful images, it lacks the personal touch that is present in human-created art. AI systems can generate endless variations of images, but they lack the individual style and technique that is present in human-created art.

The art-making process also allows the artist to experiment and take risks. When an artist is creating their work, they can try new techniques, take risks, and explore new ideas. This experimentation and risk-taking is an important aspect of the art-making process, and it allows the artist to grow and develop as an artist.

In conclusion, the art-making process is an important aspect of the art world, and it is something that AI-generated art cannot replicate. The process of creating art is not just about creating a final product, but it is also about exploring and learning, using unique techniques and styles, and taking risks. The art-making process is what makes art unique and special, and it is something that will always be valued in the art world.

Chapter 15

Artists play a crucial role in society, and they have been doing so for centuries. They serve as a voice for the voiceless, they challenge societal norms, and they provide a window into different perspectives and experiences.

Artists can communicate ideas and emotions that words cannot express. Through their work, they can touch the hearts and minds of their audience and evoke strong emotional responses. This emotional connection is what sets artists apart from other professionals, and it is what makes art so powerful.

In addition to emotional expression, artists also play an important role in social and political commentary. Throughout history, artists have used their work to comment on current events, to challenge societal norms, and to bring attention to important issues. This role is especially important in times of social and political unrest, as artists can provide a unique perspective and bring attention to important issues.

Artists also play an important role in education and cultural preservation. They provide a window into the past and help to preserve cultural heritage and traditions. This is especially important in communities where cultural traditions are threatened, as artists can keep these traditions alive through their work.

Moreover, artists provide a source of inspiration for others. They inspire others to be creative, to think outside of the box, and to explore new ideas. Through their work, artists can inspire others to see the world in a new way, and to appreciate the beauty and power of art.

Despite the important role that artists play in society, they often face challenges and obstacles. Many artists struggle to make a living, and they are often undervalued and underpaid for their work.

Additionally, the art world can be competitive and difficult to navigate, and artists may struggle to get their work seen and recognized.

Despite these challenges, artists continue to play a crucial role in society, and their work will always be valued and appreciated. Whether through emotional expression, social and political commentary, cultural preservation, or inspiration, artists play an important role in shaping our world and enriching our lives.

In conclusion, artists play a vital role in society, and their work is essential to our cultural heritage and our emotional well-being. Despite the challenges that they face, artists will continue to make a difference, to inspire others, and to play a crucial role in shaping our world.

Chapter 16

Human perception is a complex and fascinating process that sets us apart from other species and from artificial intelligence. Our ability to perceive the world around us is what gives us a sense of reality and allows us to experience the world in our own unique way.

One of the key aspects of human perception is our ability to experience emotions. Our emotions play a critical role in how we perceive and respond to the world around us. They allow us to experience pleasure and pain, happiness and sadness, and a range of other emotions that shape our experiences and our memories.

Another unique quality of human perception is our ability to experience empathy. Empathy allows us to understand and share the emotions of others, and it is a critical component of our social interactions and relationships. Our ability to experience empathy helps us to connect with others, to form meaningful relationships, and to build a sense of community.

In addition to emotions and empathy, human perception is also shaped by our individual experiences, perspectives, and biases. Our experiences and perspectives shape how we interpret and respond to the world around us, and they play a critical role in shaping our perception. Our biases, on the other hand, can influence how we perceive others and can lead to misunderstandings and conflicts.

Art is another way in which human perception is unique. Artists have the ability to use their creative skills to bring their perceptions of the world to life, and to share their perspectives with others. This ability to create art is what sets artists apart from other professionals, and it is what makes art such a powerful tool for emotional expression and cultural preservation.

Another unique quality of human perception is our ability to appreciate beauty. Our ability to appreciate beauty is what makes art such a powerful tool for emotional expression, and it is what allows us to experience the world in a profound and meaningful way. Whether it is the beauty of nature, the beauty of art, or the beauty of human experience, our ability to appreciate beauty is what makes us human.

Despite these unique qualities of human perception, it is important to acknowledge that our perception is not perfect. Our emotions, experiences, and biases can influence our perception in ways that lead to misunderstandings and conflicts. Additionally, our perception can be influenced by cultural and societal norms, which can limit our ability to see the world from different perspectives.

In conclusion, human perception is a complex and fascinating process that sets us apart from other species and from artificial intelligence. Our ability to experience emotions, empathy, and beauty, as well as our individual experiences and perspectives, shape how we perceive and respond to the world around us. While our perception is not perfect, it is what makes us human, and it is what allows us to experience the world in a profound and meaningful way.

Chapter 17

Art is often seen as a form of experimentation and risk-taking, and it is this aspect of art that sets it apart from many other forms of expression. Artists are constantly pushing boundaries and exploring new ideas, and they are not afraid to take risks to create something truly unique and meaningful.

Experimentation is a critical component of the creative process. It allows artists to explore new techniques and ideas, to push the boundaries of what is possible, and to create works of art that are truly original and innovative. Experimentation is also a form of risk-taking, as artists often venture into uncharted territory and take risks that others might not.

The process of experimentation and risk-taking is not limited to the actual creation of art. Artists also take risks in how they present their work and how they share it with the world. They may choose to showcase their work in unconventional venues, or they may choose to explore new and untested mediums or techniques.

Despite the risks involved in experimentation and risk-taking, it is these very risks that allow artists to create something truly unique and meaningful. By pushing boundaries and exploring new ideas, artists can create works of art that challenge us, that inspire us, and that evoke emotions and thought.

Another aspect of experimentation and risk-taking in art is the willingness of artists to embrace failure. In the creative process, failure is often seen as a necessary step in the journey towards success. Artists understand that not every experiment will be a success, and they are willing to embrace failure and learn from their mistakes.

Art is also a powerful tool for social and cultural change. Artists often use their works to raise awareness about important social and political issues, and to challenge societal norms and conventions. Through experimentation and risk-taking, artists can create works that provoke thought and encourage change.

In conclusion, the art of experimentation and risk-taking is a critical component of the creative process, and it is what sets art apart from many other forms of expression. By embracing failure, pushing boundaries, and exploring new ideas, artists can create works of art that are truly original and meaningful, and that have the power to inspire, challenge, and evoke change.

Chapter 18

Human experience is incredibly diverse and multifaceted. No two people experience the world in the same way, and this diversity is reflected in the art that people create. Each work of art is a unique expression of the artist's own experiences, perspectives, and emotions.

Art has the power to connect people across cultures and time, to transcend language and cultural barriers, and to help us understand the experiences of others. This is particularly true in a world that is becoming increasingly diverse and globalized, where people from all over the world are brought into close contact with one another.

Art can serve as a bridge between cultures, helping to build understanding and appreciation for different experiences and perspectives. Whether it is through visual art, literature, music, or dance, art provides a window into the diverse experiences and emotions of people from all over the world.

In addition to reflecting the diversity of human experience, art also has the power to shape and influence our experiences. Whether it is through the images and ideas that are presented, or through the emotional impact of a work of art, art could shape our thoughts, emotions, and perspectives.

One of the key benefits of diversity in art is that it provides a platform for underrepresented groups to share their experiences and perspectives with a wider audience. This can help to promote understanding and respect for different cultures and communities and can help to build a more inclusive and equitable society.

The diversity of human experience is also reflected in the different art forms that exist, each of which speaks to different aspects of human experience. Whether it is through the visual expression of painting and sculpture, the emotional impact of music and dance, or the imaginative worlds of literature and film, art provides a rich and diverse tapestry of human experience.

In conclusion, the diversity of human experience is a critical component of the art world, and it is what gives art its unique power and impact. Whether it is through the reflection of different experiences and perspectives, or through the shaping and influencing of our experiences, art could connect us to one another, to help us understand and appreciate the experiences of others, and to promote a more inclusive and equitable world.

Chapter 19

Art has always been an integral part of human culture and society, playing a critical role in shaping the beliefs, values, and identities of individuals and communities. From ancient cave paintings to contemporary street art, art has served as a reflection of the times and a powerful tool for communication and expression.

Art has the power to capture and express the essence of a particular time, place, and culture. It provides a visual record of human history and helps us to understand the beliefs, values, and experiences of different societies and cultures.

For example, the art of ancient civilizations like the Egyptians, Greeks, and Romans provides a window into the beliefs, values, and experiences of these societies, and gives us a glimpse into their religious, political, and cultural systems. Similarly, the art of medieval Europe provides insight into the feudal system and the power structures of the time, while the art of the Renaissance reflects the cultural and intellectual awakening of Europe in the 15th and 16th centuries.

Art also plays a critical role in shaping cultural identity, providing a visual representation of a particular culture or community. For example, indigenous art has played a critical role in preserving the cultural heritage of indigenous communities, and in many cases, has been used as a tool for cultural resistance and assertion. Similarly, the art of immigrant communities often reflects their experiences of migration, adaptation, and identity, and helps to preserve their cultural heritage in their new home.

In addition to reflecting and shaping cultural identity, art also has the power to bring people together, fostering a sense of community and belonging. Whether it is through shared cultural experiences, like visiting a museum or attending a concert, or through the creation of new communities, like online art communities, art has the power to bring people together and create a sense of shared identity and purpose.

Art is also a powerful tool for communication, providing a way for individuals and communities to express their ideas, beliefs, and values to a wider audience. Whether it is through political art, like protest posters and murals, or by art in advertising and propaganda, art has the power to shape public opinion and influence social and political change.

The cultural significance of art cannot be overstated. Art reflects the times, a powerful tool for communication, and a way to preserve and shape cultural identity. Whether it is through its ability to capture the essence of a particular time, place, and culture, or through its power to bring people together and foster a sense of community, art can enrich our lives and to shape the world around us.

In conclusion, the cultural significance of art is a critical component of the art world, and it is what gives art its unique power and impact. Whether it is through its ability to reflect and shape cultural identity, to bring people together, or to communicate ideas and values, art can enrich our lives, foster a sense of community, and shape the world around us.

Chapter 20

Artificial Intelligence has made tremendous advancements in recent years, and its impact on the art world has been particularly notable. Midjourney AI, a tool that creates artificial art through prompts, has garnered attention and sparked debates about the future of traditional artists and the art industry. However, despite its impressive abilities, there are still limitations to what AI can achieve in terms of creativity.

One of the biggest limitations of AI is its lack of imagination. Unlike human artists, AI does not have the capacity for free-thinking or independent thought. Instead, it relies on pre-existing data and algorithms to generate art. This means that AI can only create art that is based on what it has already seen or learned, and it cannot come up with completely new and original ideas.

Another limitation of AI is its lack of emotional connection to the art it creates. Human artists have a unique and personal connection to their work, often driven by their experiences, emotions, and cultural background. This emotional connection is what gives art its power and significance, and it is something that AI cannot replicate.

In addition, AI can also struggle with understanding and incorporating cultural context into its art. While it may be able to generate visually impressive works, it lacks the cultural knowledge and awareness that human artists bring to the table. This can result in artificial art that is lacking in depth and meaning, and that fails to resonate with audiences.

Finally, AI also lacks the ability to truly understand the creative process. The act of artmaking is not just about the result, but about the journey of discovery and experimentation that leads to it. Human artists could experiment, make mistakes, and take risks in their work, whereas AI simply follows a set of programmed rules.

In conclusion, while AI has made impressive advancements in the realm of art, it still has limitations that prevent it from fully taking over the role of traditional artists. Human creativity, imagination, emotional connection, cultural awareness, and understanding of the creative process are all unique qualities that AI cannot replicate. These qualities are what give art its power and significance, and they are what make it a truly human experience.

Chapter 21

Art has always been a powerful tool for human self-expression. It allows individuals to express their thoughts, emotions, and experiences in a way that words cannot. Throughout history, art has been used as a means of conveying political messages, exploring personal struggles, and capturing the beauty of the world around us.

For artists, the act of creating art is a form of self-expression that is both personal and universal. When an artist creates a piece of art, they are expressing their innermost thoughts, feelings, and experiences in a way that is unique to them. However, the art they create also can connect with and resonate with others, creating a universal understanding and connection.

This connection between the artist and the audience is one of the defining qualities of art. When people view a piece of art, they are not just seeing a physical object, but a representation of the artist's soul. The art speaks to the viewer, communicating a message or emotion that transcends language and cultural boundaries.

For many artists, the act of creating art is also a therapeutic process. It allows them to process their emotions and experiences, and to make sense of the world around them. This is why art is often seen as a form of self-expression that is both personal and transformative.

However, while AI-generated art may be visually impressive, it cannot replicate the personal and transformative nature of human-created art. AI-generated art is not the result of a personal journey or an emotional connection, but rather a set of algorithms and data. This means that AI-generated art lacks the depth and meaning that comes from the artist's personal experiences and emotions.

In conclusion, art as a form of self-expression is a fundamental aspect of the human experience. Whether it is used as a means of exploring personal struggles, conveying political messages, or simply capturing the beauty of the world around us, art can connect with and resonate with others. The personal and transformative nature of art is what makes it a truly human experience, and it is something that AI cannot replicate.

Chapter 22

As technology continues to advance and shape our world, it's no surprise that it has also made its mark in the art world. Artificial intelligence has the potential to revolutionize the way art is created, but it also raises questions about the role of technology in artmaking.

In this chapter, we'll explore the intersection of art and technology and how AI is changing the game. From digital art to interactive installations, artists are finding new and innovative ways to use technology in their work. Some view AI as a tool to enhance their creativity, while others see it as a threat to the traditional art-making process.

One example of how technology is changing the art world is through virtual and augmented reality. Artists can now create immersive experiences for viewers that blur the line between reality and the digital world. These experiences can be interactive, allowing the audience to participate and engage with the art in new ways.

However, it's important to note that while technology has the potential to enhance the art-making process, it also has limitations. There is only so much that AI can do, and ultimately, it is the human touch and creative intuition that gives art its emotional depth and meaning.

Artists must also consider the ethical implications of using technology in their work. With the rise of AI, it raises the question of whether it is ethical to use it to create art that is sold as original and handmade. The answer is not a clear-cut one, and it's up to each individual artist to decide what works best for them.

In conclusion, the intersection of art and technology offers exciting possibilities for the future of artmaking. While it's important to consider the limitations and ethical implications of using AI, it can also inspire new forms of creativity and offer artists new ways to express themselves.

Chapter 23

As technology continues to evolve, it's becoming increasingly important for artists to stay ahead of the curve and lead the way in the innovation of artmaking. The traditional art world can be slow to embrace new technology and ideas, so it's up to artists to push the boundaries and find new ways to use technology in their work.

Artists have a unique perspective and understanding of their medium, and they are in a prime position to experiment and create new forms of expression. Whether it's through digital art, virtual reality, or interactive installations, artists are finding new and exciting ways to use technology in their work.

Innovation in the art world not only advances the medium, but it also opens new opportunities for artists. By embracing technology, artists can reach new audiences and create work that resonates with a wider audience. It also allows artists to express their ideas in new and exciting ways, pushing the boundaries of what is possible.

However, it's important for artists to approach innovation with caution. The use of technology in art can be a double-edged sword, and it's up to each artist to decide what works best for them. Artists must weigh the potential benefits of using technology against the limitations and ethical implications of doing so.

Artists must also be mindful of how they present their work and how it's perceived by the public. With the rise of AI, there's a growing concern that technology will replace the traditional art-making process and lead to the loss of jobs for artists. It's important for artists to educate the public about the role of technology in art and how it can be used to enhance, not replace, the art-making process.

In conclusion, artist-led innovation is critical in the advancement of the art world. Artists have the unique perspective and creativity to lead the way in the innovation of artmaking, and it's up to them to decide how to best use technology in their work. Whether it's through digital art, virtual reality, or interactive installations, artists have the power to shape the future of the art world.

Chapter 24

As technology continues to advance, the use of artificial intelligence in the world of art has become increasingly prevalent. While some view AI as a threat to traditional artists and the art world, others see it as a tool for inspiration and collaboration.

One of the biggest concerns about AI in the art world is its potential to replace human artists and devalue the work that they create. However, it's important to remember that AI is not capable of replicating the unique qualities of human perception and experience. No matter how advanced technology becomes, it will never be able to fully replicate the emotional connection and cultural significance that artists bring to their work.

Despite this, the integration of AI in the art world is not going away. In fact, it's likely that it will continue to play an increasingly important role in the future of art and creativity. But the key to ensuring that AI is used in a way that benefits artists and the art world is to ensure that artists remain at the forefront of innovation.

Artists have always been at the forefront of experimentation and risk-taking, and this is no different when it comes to the intersection of art and technology. By embracing AI and using it as a tool for inspiration and collaboration, artists can continue to push the boundaries of what's possible in the world of art.

The future of art and AI is still uncertain, but one thing is clear: the role of artists in society will continue to be crucial. Through their unique perspectives and experiences, artists have the power to shape the way that we understand and interact with the world around us. Whether working with AI or not, the art that artists create will always have the power to evoke emotions, challenge cultural norms, and inspire change.

Chapter 25

As we reach the end of this journey exploring the relationship between Midjourney AI and traditional artists, it's clear that the future of art and technology is still an open question. There's no doubt that AI will play an increasingly significant role in the world of art, but the role of human artists is far from over.

Art has always been a human endeavor, a way for us to express our emotions, thoughts, and experiences. AI, while able to produce impressive and intricate works, lacks the personal touch, the unique perspective, and the emotional connection that human artists bring to their work. In many ways, the human touch is what gives art its value.

The future of art education will also play a significant role in determining the place of human artists in the years to come. If artists can embrace technology and incorporate it into their creative processes, they will remain relevant and vital to the world of art. If they resist technology and reject its place in their craft, they risk being left behind.

Artists, who are known for taking risks and experimenting, have the power to lead the charge in the intersection of art and technology. They can harness the power of AI to create new and innovative works, while still maintaining their human perspective and creativity. By embracing technology and staying at the forefront of innovation, artists will continue to have a vital role in shaping the future of art.

The art market will also play a role in the future of human artists. As AI-generated art becomes more prevalent, it's likely that the market for traditional art will continue to evolve. However, it's important to remember that the value of art goes beyond just financial gain. Art has the power to evoke emotions, connect people, and provide a unique window into the human experience. These are qualities that AI will never be able to replicate.

Finally, it's important to remember the cultural significance of art. Art has the power to reflect and shape our society and the values we hold dear. Human artists bring a unique perspective and voice to this conversation, and their contributions are critical to ensuring that art remains a meaningful and relevant part of our culture.

In conclusion, while AI may be able to create impressive works of art, it will never be able to replace the human touch, the personal connection, and the cultural significance that human artists bring to their work. The continued relevance of human artists is ensured by their unique qualities, creativity, and ability to innovate. The future of art is not about choosing between AI and human artists, but rather about finding a way for these two elements to coexist and collaborate in meaningful and impactful ways.

Thank You

The End

www.ingramcontent.com/pod-product-compliance
Lightning Source LLC
Chambersburg PA
CBHW070321220526
45465CB00013B/2057